INSTANT TEST PREP

Common Core Mathematics

Math Practice Test

Grade 3

© 2021 by C. Hawas

ISBN 9798719662145

Acknowledgements

Thank you to the following sources for providing graphs, charts, diagrams, and illustrations.

Evil Math Wizard
www.teacherspayteachers.com/Store/Evil-Math-Wizard

Innovative Teaching Ideas
www.teacherspayteachers.com/Store/Innovative-Teaching-Ideas

Hidesy's Clipart
www.teacherspayteachers.com/Store/Hidesys-Clipart

Teacher Trap
www.teacherspayteachers.com/Store/Teacher-Trap

Teaches Third in Georgia
www.teacherspayteachers.com/Store/Teachesthirdingeorgia

INTRODUCTION
For Parents, Teachers, and Tutors

About the Common Core State Standards

- The Common Core State Standards describe all the skills that students need.
- Forty-one states have adopted the standards.
- Those states that have adopted the standards have state tests based on the Common Core skills.

About this Book

- This book contains one practice test that covers every Common Core skill.
- The practice tests can be used to help prepare for any state test based on the Common Core standards.
- The practice test has 60 questions and is divided into two sessions.
- The answer key lists the skill assessed by each question.

Question Formats

- Most state tests are taken online and include a wide range of question formats.
- The tests may include multiple choice, multi-select, equation response, written response, and graphic response questions where students use online features to complete a task.
- This practice test has adapted the questions to allow simple and straightforward answers.

Instant Test Practice

- The practice test is designed to be easy to take and simple to mark.
- The test covers all the mathematics skills that students are expected to have.
- The test will prepare students for the wide range of question types on the real tests.
- The skills listed in the answer key allow missing skills to be identified and for revision to be planned accordingly.

Common Core Mathematics

Practice Test

Session 1

Instructions

Read each question carefully. For each multiple-choice question, choose the correct answer. For other types of questions, follow the directions given in the question.

1   Alice made the array below to represent a product.

Complete the missing numbers to show the array it represents.

$$\underline{\hspace{2cm}} \times \underline{\hspace{2cm}}$$

2   Which of these gives $\frac{20}{5}$ as a whole number?

   Ⓐ   3

   Ⓑ   4

   Ⓒ   5

   Ⓓ   15

3 Complete the missing numbers to find the value of 617 + 135. Write the missing numbers on the blank lines.

$$600 + \underline{\hspace{2cm}} + 10 + \underline{\hspace{2cm}} + 7 + \underline{\hspace{2cm}}$$

4 Izzy marked the fraction $\frac{6}{10}$ on a number line, as shown below.

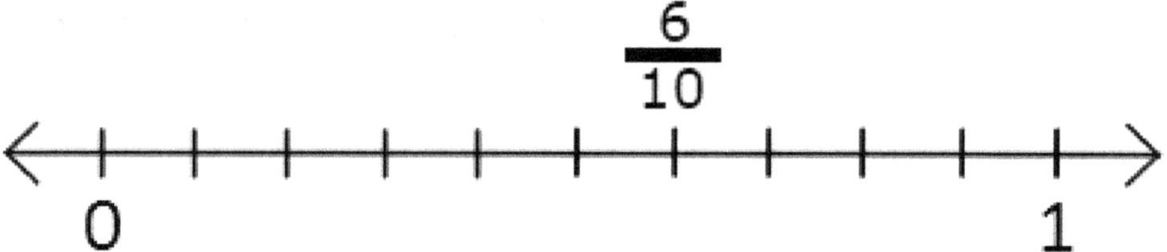

Which fraction is equivalent to $\frac{6}{10}$?

Ⓐ $\frac{3}{5}$

Ⓑ $\frac{4}{5}$

Ⓒ $\frac{3}{4}$

Ⓓ $\frac{2}{3}$

5 Alistair measured the heights of the tulips he had in a vase. The diagram below shows the heights.

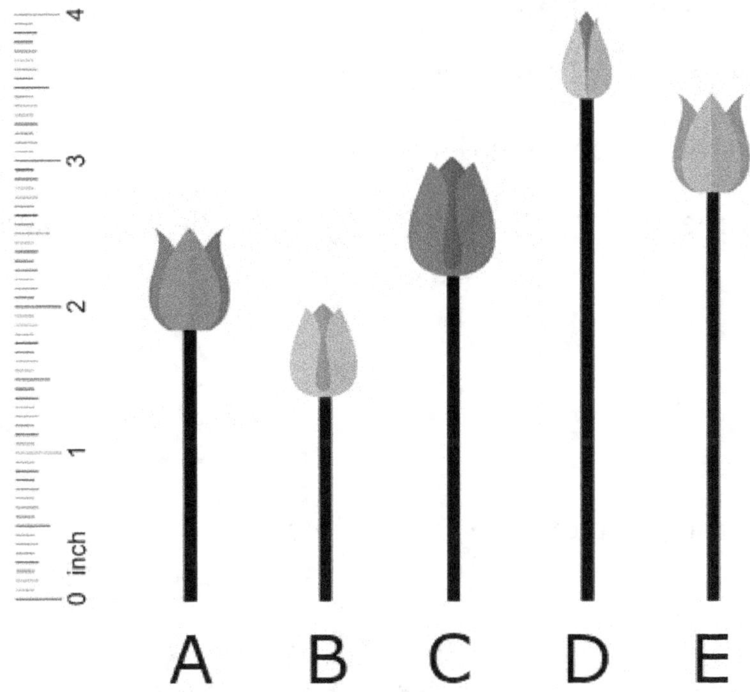

Which tulip is closest in length to 3 inches? Write the correct letter.

Answer ___________

Which tulip is about twice as long as Tulip B? Write the correct letter.

Answer ___________

What is the length of Tulip A to the nearest half inch?

Answer ___________ inches

6   A quadrilateral has 4 equal sides. Which question would determine whether it is a square or a rhombus?

    Ⓐ   How many angles does the shape have?

    Ⓑ   Does the shape have any parallel sides?

    Ⓒ   Does the shape have right angles?

    Ⓓ   How many pairs of parallel sides does the shape have?

7   Finlay cut the piece of cake shown below.

What fraction of the whole cake is the piece?

Answer ___________

8 Felix's karate class was supposed to start at 4:45 p.m. The class started 17 minutes late. What time did the class start?

Ⓐ   4:52 p.m.

Ⓑ   5:02 p.m.

Ⓒ   5:12 p.m.

Ⓓ   5:22 p.m.

9 Select **all** the expressions that are equal to 180.

Ⓐ 3×6

Ⓑ 3×6 tens

Ⓒ $3 \times 6 \times 10$

Ⓓ 6×3

Ⓔ 6×3 tens

Ⓕ   6 tens $\times$ 3 tens

10 The number 8 multiplied by what number equals 72?

Answer ___________

11 The graph below shows the number of trees of each type in Anderson Park.

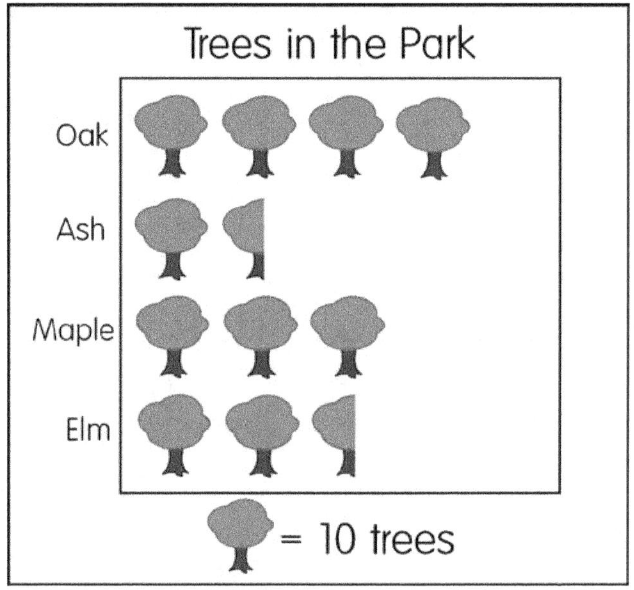

How many oak trees are there?

Answer ___________

How many ash trees are there?

Answer ___________

How many more oak trees are there than ash trees?

Answer ___________

12 Evie divided a triangle into sections, as shown below.

Which statement is true?

Ⓐ Evie divided the triangle into thirds because there are 3 parts.

Ⓑ Evie divided the triangle into thirds because the 3 parts combine to form a whole.

Ⓒ Evie did not divide the triangle into thirds because the 3 parts have different sizes.

Ⓓ Evie did not divide the triangle into thirds because there are more than 3 parts.

13 Jackson spends a total of $32 ordering pizzas for a party. Each pizza costs $8. Which expression can be used to find how many pizzas he ordered?

Ⓐ $32 + 8$

Ⓑ $32 - 8$

Ⓒ 32×8

Ⓓ $32 \div 8$

14 Select the **two** statements that are correct.

Ⓐ $\dfrac{1}{2} = \dfrac{4}{8}$

Ⓑ $\dfrac{1}{4} = \dfrac{6}{8}$

Ⓒ $\dfrac{1}{3} = \dfrac{2}{6}$

Ⓓ $\dfrac{3}{8} = \dfrac{6}{4}$

Ⓔ $\dfrac{2}{5} = \dfrac{3}{10}$

15 Write numbers in the empty boxes to show an expression equivalent to the expression below.

$$6 \times (5 + 7)$$

$$(6 \times 5) + (\square \times \square)$$

16 Clayton made four types of juice to sell at a school fair.

- He sold $\frac{5}{8}$ of the apple juice.

- He sold $\frac{3}{4}$ of the pineapple juice.

- He sold $\frac{1}{4}$ of the mango juice.

- He sold $\frac{7}{8}$ of the orange juice.

Which juice did he sell the largest fraction of?

Ⓐ apple juice

Ⓑ pineapple juice

Ⓒ mango juice

Ⓓ orange juice

17 The table shows the number of visitors to a museum each weekday for one week.

World History Museum

Day	Number of Visitors
Monday	486
Tuesday	468
Wednesday	502
Thursday	584
Friday	766

How many visitors did the museum have on Monday, rounded to the nearest ten?

Answer _______________

How many visitors did the museum have on Thursday, rounded to the nearest hundred?

Answer _______________

18 Hayley marked a fraction on a number line, as shown below.

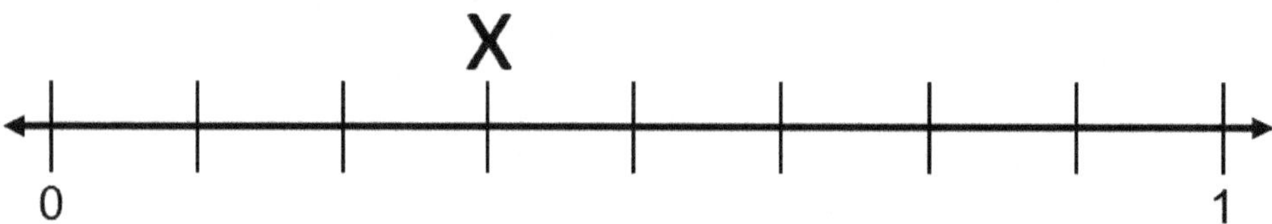

What fraction did Hayley mark?

Answer _______________

19 A number pattern starts with the number 5. Which rule to get the next number would result in a pattern where all the numbers are odd?

Ⓐ Add 3.

Ⓑ Add 4.

Ⓒ Multiply by 2.

Ⓓ Multiply by 4.

20 Jeffrey used a set of scales and weights in grams to find the mass of a jar of jelly. The diagram below shows when the scales were balanced.

What is the mass of the jar of jelly?

Answer _______________ grams

21 Frankie swims 8 laps of a pool. Each lap has a distance of 40 feet. What is the total distance that Frankie swims?

Ⓐ   240 feet

Ⓑ   320 feet

Ⓒ   360 feet

Ⓓ   420 feet

22 Camilla covers the poster below with 1-inch squares.

She covers it with 9 rows of 9 squares each. There are no gaps or overlaps. Which statement is true about the poster?

Ⓐ   It has a length of 81 inches.

Ⓑ   It has a height of 81 inches.

Ⓒ   It has a perimeter of 81 inches.

Ⓓ   It has an area of 81 square inches.

23 Cecilia wants to stick on a border around the 4 edges of a mirror.

The mirror is 30 inches wide and 50 inches high. How long will the border need to be to go around the 4 edges?

Answer __________ inches

24 A baker makes a total of 386 muffins one morning. He sells 247 muffins during the day. Round each number to the nearest 10 to estimate how many muffins he has left at the end of the day.

__________ − __________ = __________

25   Jarvis wants to solve the equation below.

$$\square \div 6 = 42$$

Which expression could be used to find the missing number?

Ⓐ 42×6

Ⓑ $42 \div 6$

Ⓒ $42 + 6$

Ⓓ $42 - 6$

26   A table tennis court is shown below.

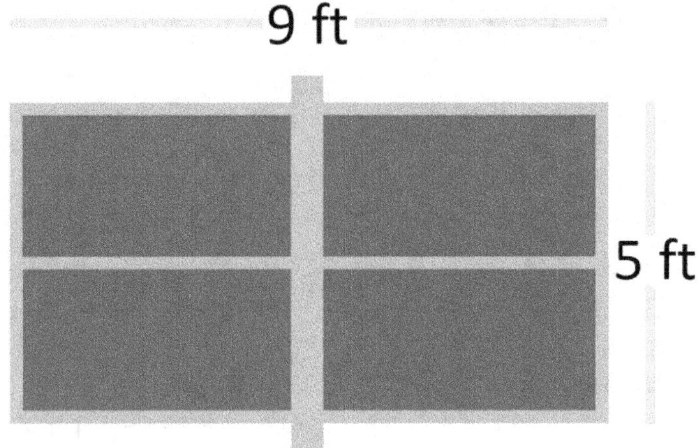

Which of these shows how to find the area of the court, in square feet?

Ⓐ 9×5

Ⓑ $9 + 5$

Ⓒ $2 \times (9 \times 5)$

Ⓓ $2 \times (9 + 5)$

27   Alisha has a total of 75 bread rolls. She divides all the bread rolls into baskets of 5 rolls each. How many baskets of bread rolls will she have?

Answer _______________

28   Which clock shows the time 3:20?

29   Complete the equation with the number that makes the equation true.

$$35 = \underline{\hspace{1.5cm}} \times 5$$

30   Jarvis made a graph to show the types of stores in his local mall.

How many clothing stores are there?

Answer ____________

How many hobby stores are there?

Answer ____________

How many more clothing stores are there than hobby stores?

Answer ____________

Common Core Mathematics

Practice Test

Session 2

31   A teacher places notebooks in equal piles, as shown below.

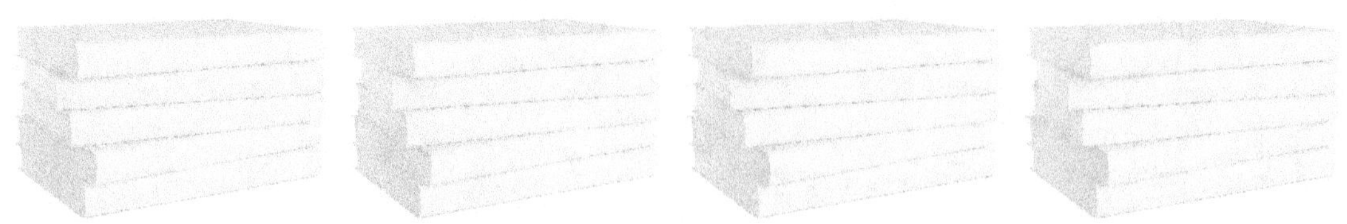

Which expression represents the total number of notebooks?

Ⓐ   4 × 4

Ⓑ   4 × 5

Ⓒ   4 + 4

Ⓓ   4 + 5

32   Write the correct number in each box to create a fraction equal to 4.

33 Select **all** the situations that can be represented by 40 ÷ 10.

Ⓐ The 40 students going kayaking were sorted into 10 equal groups.

Ⓑ Ben warmed up for 10 minutes and then swam laps for 40 minutes.

Ⓒ Ben bought a backpack for $40 and received a $10 discount.

Ⓓ A bus carrying 40 students had 10 empty seats.

Ⓔ The 40 chairs in a cafeteria were placed equally around 10 tables.

Ⓕ Ben's baseball team washed 40 cars and charged $10 for each car.

34 Sara has a ballet class that starts at the time shown below.

What time does Sara's ballet class start?

Answer ______ : ______

35 A multiplication table is shown below.

X	0	1	2	3	4	5	6	7	8	9	10
0	0	0	0	0	0	0	0	0	0	0	0
1	0	1	2	3	4	5	6	7	8	9	10
2	0	2	4	6	8	10	12	14	16	18	20
3	0	3	6	9	12	15	18	21	24	27	30
4	0	4	8	12	16	20	24	28	32	36	40
5	0	5	10	15	20	25	30	35	40	45	50
6	0	6	12	18	24	30	36	42	48	54	60
7	0	7	14	21	28	35	42	49	56	63	70
8	0	8	16	24	32	40	48	56	64	72	80
9	0	9	18	27	36	45	54	63	72	81	90
10	0	10	20	30	40	50	60	70	80	90	100

Based on the table, which of these is a multiple of 7?

Ⓐ 36

Ⓑ 46

Ⓒ 56

Ⓓ 66

36 Cora has 4 piles containing 5 dimes each and 6 piles containing 10 nickels each. How many coins does Cora have in all?

Answer ___________

37 The diagram below represents 1 inch.

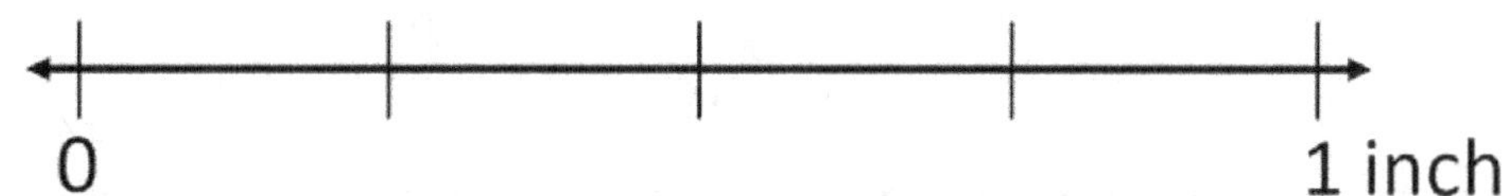

Which point on the number line represents $\frac{1}{4}$ inches?

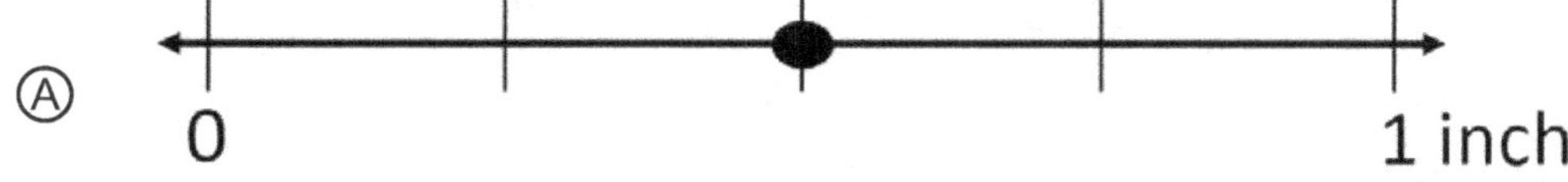

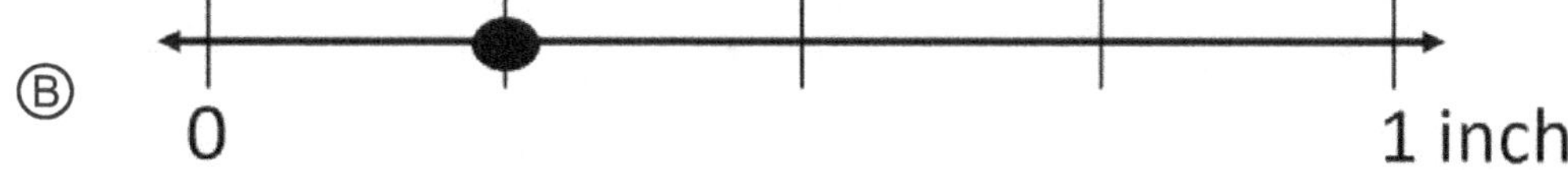

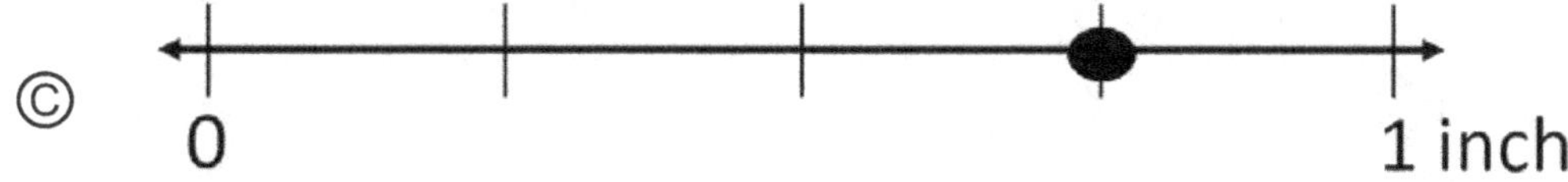

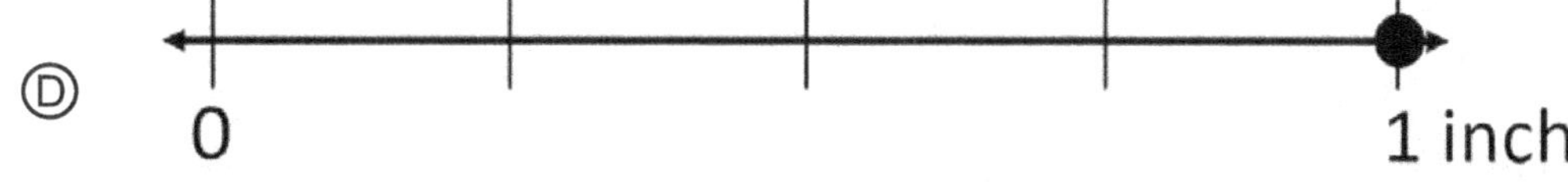

38 Which number is 780 when rounded to the nearest 10?

Ⓐ 768

Ⓑ 772

Ⓒ 776

Ⓓ 788

39 Esther has the amount of liquid plant food shown below.

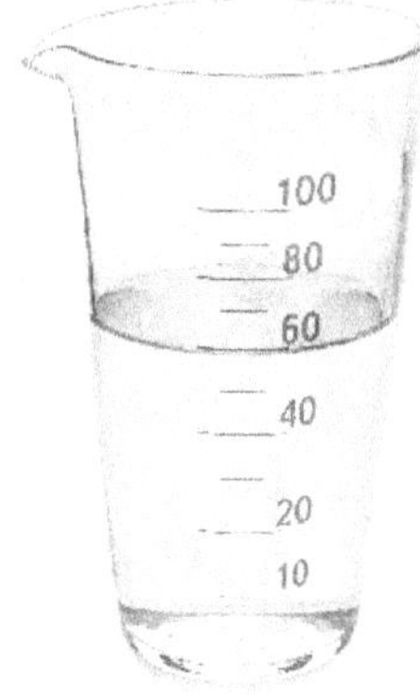

She divides the plant food equally among 3 plants. How much does she feed each plant?

Ⓐ 20 mL

Ⓑ 30 mL

Ⓒ 60 mL

Ⓓ 180 mL

40 Lenny made the diagram below to show the distance his family drove to go on vacation from Woodville to Paxton.

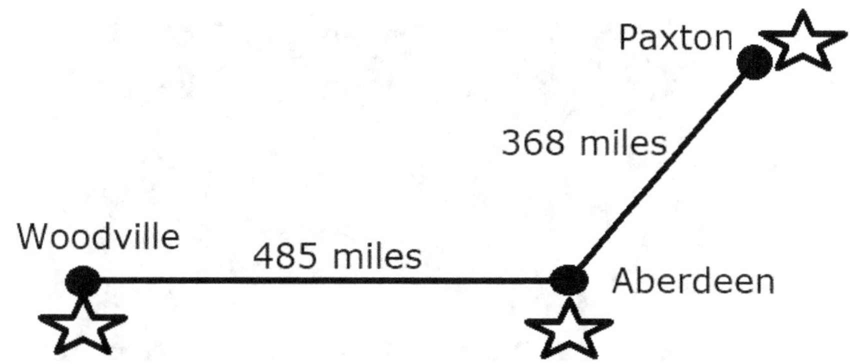

How far did the family drive from Woodville to Paxton?

Answer ____________ miles

41 Sophia draws a rectangle with an area of 80 square centimeters. The height of the rectangle is 10 centimeters. What is the width of the rectangle?

Answer ____________ centimeters

42 The base of the fish tank below has a length of 20 inches and a width of 6 inches.

Write an expression that uses multiplication to find the area of the base, in square inches.

_________ × _________

What is the area of the base?

Answer __________ square inches

43 Danielle makes and sells bars of soap. She sells each bar of soap for the same price. The table below shows the amount she makes for different numbers of bars.

Danielle's Sales

Number of Bars	Amount Made
2	$6
4	$12
5	$15
6	$18
8	?

How much does Danielle sell each bar of soap for?

Answer $____________

How much would Danielle sell 8 bars of soap for?

Answer $____________

44 Write the correct number in each box to write two fractions equivalent to $\frac{2}{3}$.

$$\frac{2}{3} = \frac{\Box}{6} = \frac{\Box}{12}$$

45 The fraction $\frac{4}{6}$ is shaded below.

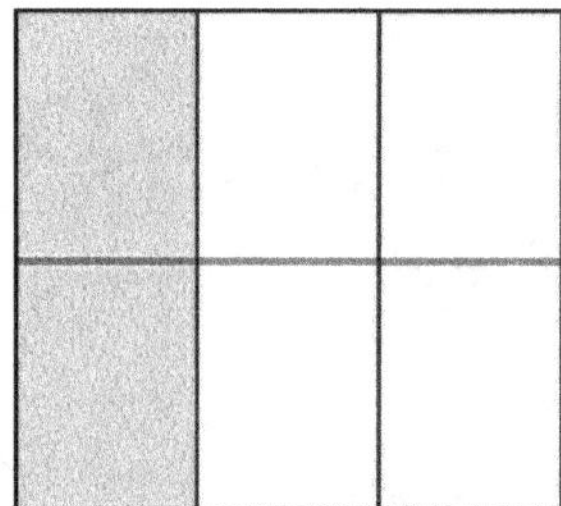

Which of these has the same fraction of the rectangle shaded?

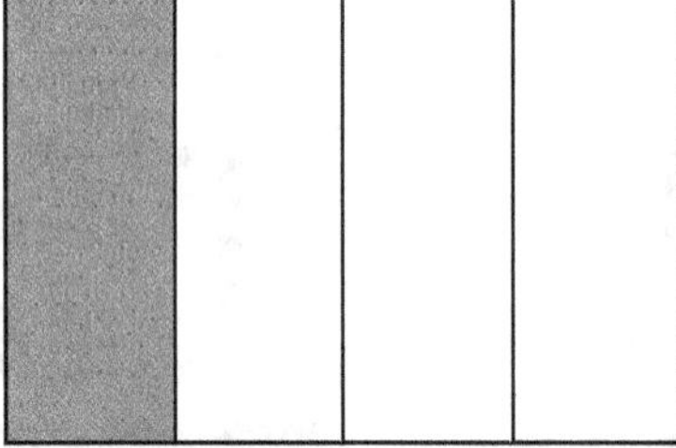

46 A square is divided into sections. Four different sections are shaded and labeled A through D, as shown below.

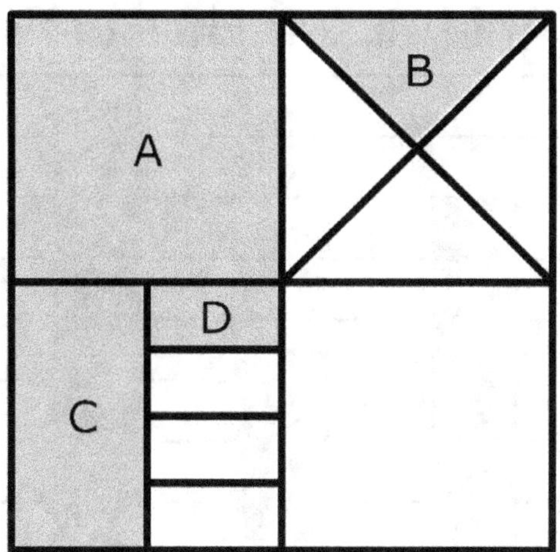

Which shaded section makes up $\frac{1}{4}$ of the shape? Write the letter for the section.

Answer _____________

Which shaded section makes up $\frac{1}{8}$ of the shape? Write the letter for the section.

Answer _____________

47   The graph below shows the numbers of animals of each type on a farm.

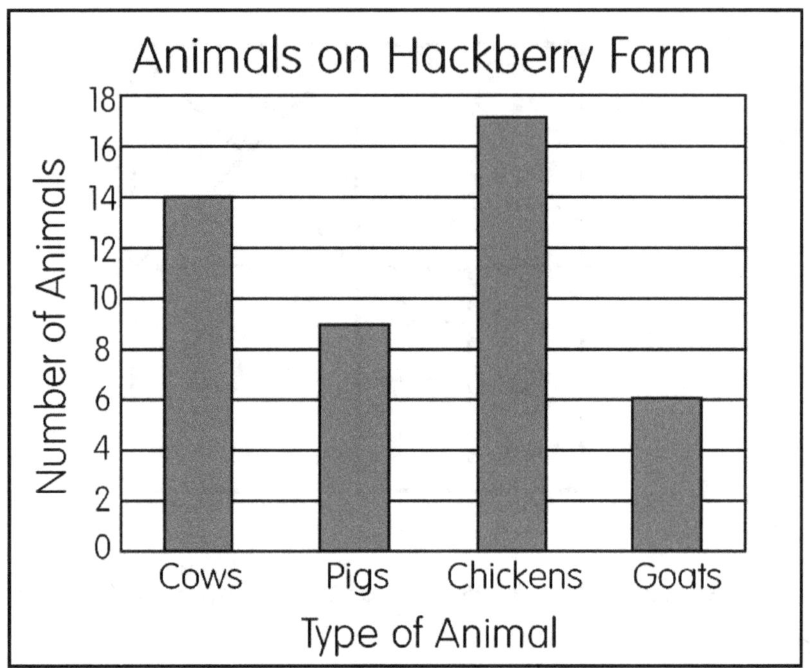

How many cows are there?

Answer ______________

How many more chickens are there than pigs?

Answer ______________

How many pigs and goats are there combined?

Answer ______________

48 Vivian has the piece of ribbon shown below.

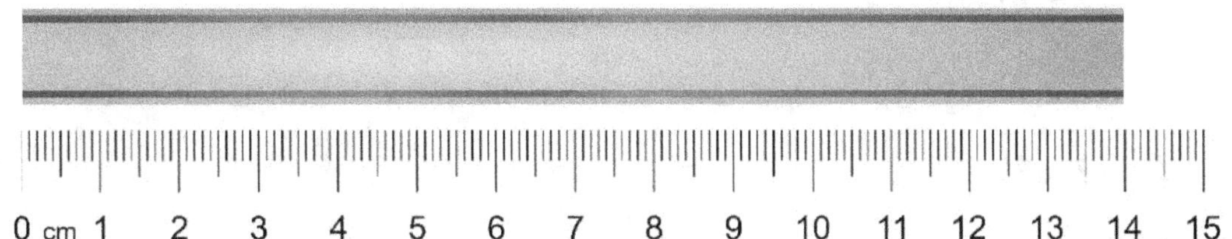

Vivian cuts off a 6 centimeter piece of ribbon. Vivian then cuts the remaining ribbon in half. Which expression can be used to find the length of each equal piece of ribbon, in centimeters?

Ⓐ $(14 \div 2) - 6$

Ⓑ $(14 \times 2) - 6$

Ⓒ $(14 - 6) \div 2$

Ⓓ $(14 - 6) \times 2$

49 What fraction is represented by point Q on the number line shown?

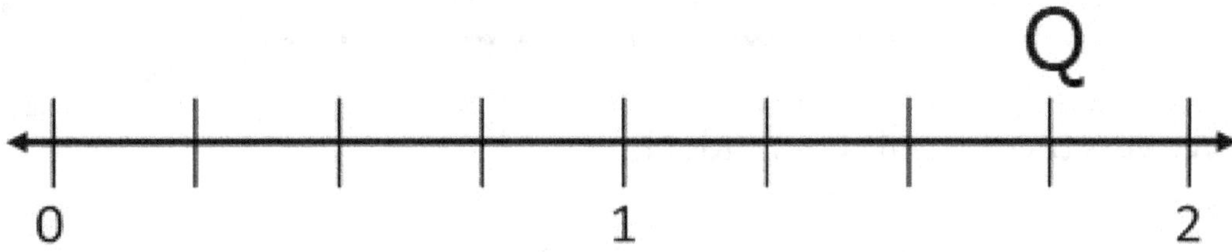

Answer ___________

50 Which expression is equivalent to $7 \times (3 + 2)$?

Ⓐ $(7 + 3) \times (7 + 2)$

Ⓑ $(7 \times 3) + (7 \times 2)$

Ⓒ $(7 \times 3) + 2$

Ⓓ $(7 \times 3) \times 2$

51 Courtney drew the diagram below to represent the area of a paddock on her farm. Each square represent 1 square yard.

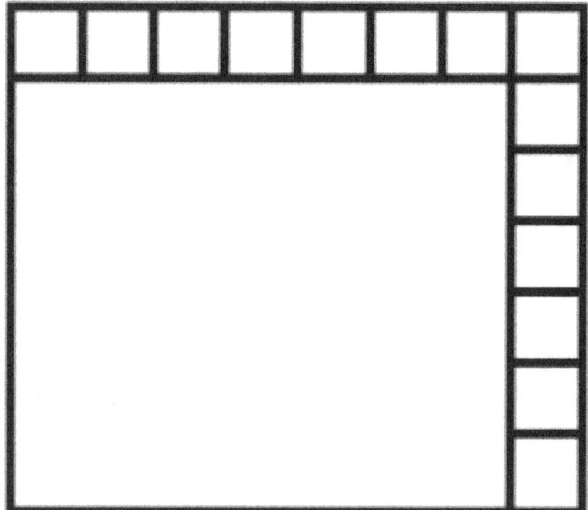

What is the area of the paddock?

Answer _______________ square yards

52 Brent has a kid's puzzle made of pieces of different shapes, as shown below.

Which **two** types of quadrilaterals form part of the house?

Ⓐ kite

Ⓑ rectangle

Ⓒ rhombus

Ⓓ square

Ⓔ trapezoid

53 Four fractions are listed below.

$$\frac{1}{3}, \ \frac{1}{8}, \ \frac{1}{6}, \ \frac{1}{5}$$

Which fraction is the greatest?

Answer ___________

54   What number makes both equations true?

$$8 \times \square = 32$$

$$32 \div \square = 8$$

Answer ______________

55   Rowena measured the size of a playground and drew the diagram below to shows its dimensions.

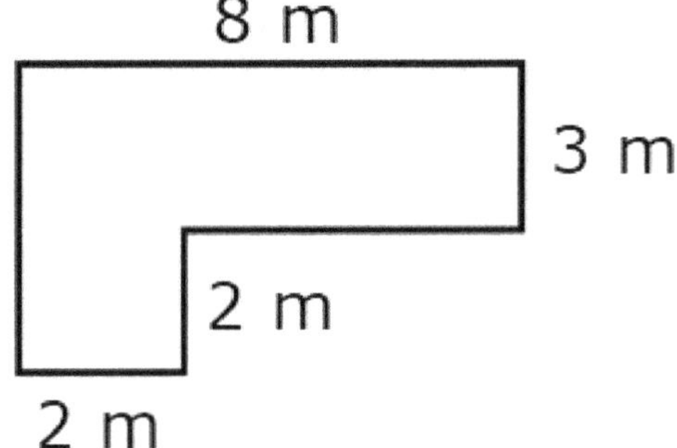

Complete the expression that could be used to find the total area of the playground, in square meters.

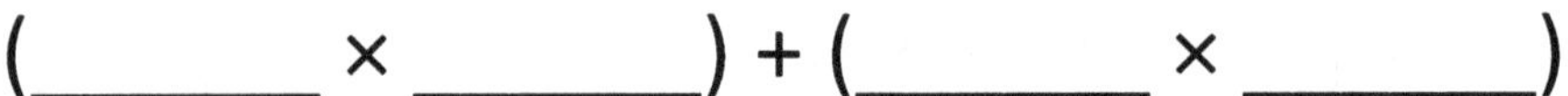

$$(\underline{\hspace{2cm}} \times \underline{\hspace{2cm}}) + (\underline{\hspace{2cm}} \times \underline{\hspace{2cm}})$$

What is the total area of the playground?

Answer ______________ square meters

56 For each equation, write a pair of numbers in the empty boxes to make a correct equation. Use a different pair of numbers for each equation.

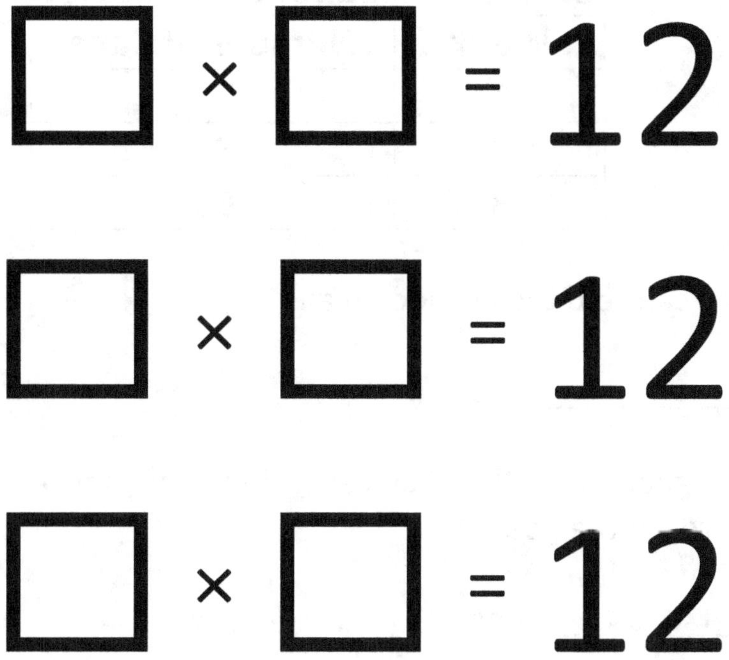

57 What is the value of 90×10?

Ⓐ 900

Ⓑ 990

Ⓒ 9,000

Ⓓ 9,900

58 Adriana's class collected cans for a food drive. The table shows how many cans they collected each week.

Cans Collected for a Food Drive

Week	Number of Cans
1	71
2	58
3	63

How many cans did they collect in all?

Answer ____________ cans

The class's goal is to collect 300 cans. How many more cans do they need to collect to reach the goal?

Answer ____________ cans

59 The dimensions of 6 rectangles are given below, in inches. Which rectangle has the greatest perimeter?

Ⓐ 6 by 5

Ⓑ 4 by 7

Ⓒ 3 by 9

Ⓓ 7 by 6

Ⓔ 3 by 11

Ⓕ 4 by 8

60 Aaron fills a bucket with water to feed his plants. The arrow on the diagram below shows the level of water in the bucket.

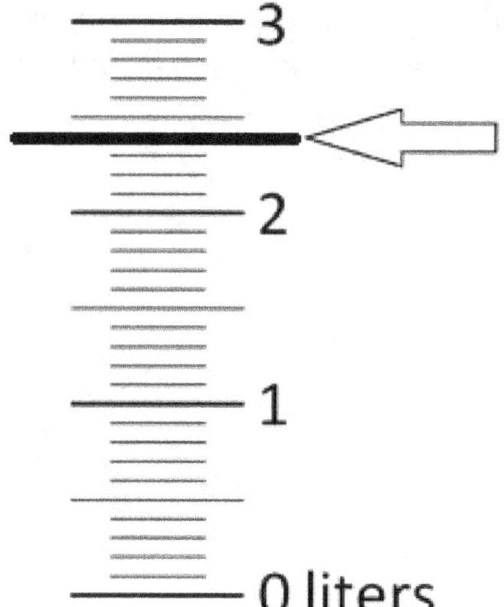

How much water does Aaron have in the bucket, to the nearest half liter?

Answer ____________ liters

ANSWER KEY

Common Core State Standards

The Common Core State Standards describe what students are expected to know and what students should be able to do at the end of each grade. They describe all the skills and knowledge that students should have. Student learning throughout the year is based on these standards, and the state tests assess these standards. All the questions in this book cover the Common Core State Standards.

Assessing Skills and Knowledge

The skills listed in the Common Core State Standards are divided into five topics, or clusters. These are:

- Operations and Algebraic Thinking
- Number and Operations in Base Ten
- Number and Operations – Fractions
- Measurement and Data
- Geometry

Within each topic, the specific math skills are listed and numbered. The answer key lists the standard code for each skill. The answer key also includes a short summary of the skill assessed by each question.

Common Core Mathematics Practice Test, Session 1

Question	Answer	Standard	Skill Summary
1	4×3	3.OA.1	interpret products of whole numbers
2	B	3.NF.3.c	express whole numbers as fractions
3	100, 30, 5	3.NBT.2	add and subtract whole numbers
4	A	3.NF.3.a	understand equivalent fractions
5	C, D, 2½	3.MD.4	measure length and show data on line plots
6	C	3.G.1	recognize, categorize, and analyze shapes
7	$\frac{1}{8}$	3.NF.1	understand fractions
8	B	3.MD.1	write time and solve time problems
9	B, C, E	3.NBT.3	multiply numbers by multiples of 10
10	9	3.OA.6	understand division as an unknown-factor problem
11	40, 15, 25	3.MD.3	draw picture and bar graphs and solve problems
12	C	3.G.2	partition shapes into parts and relate to fractions
13	D	3.OA.2	interpret quotients of whole numbers
14	A, C	3.NF.3.b	recognize and generate equivalent fractions
15	6, 7	3.OA.5	use properties of operations to multiply and divide
16	D	3.NF.3.d	compare fractions
17	490, 600	3.NBT.1	round whole numbers
18	$\frac{3}{8}$	3.NF.2	represent fractions on a number line
19	B	3.OA.9	identify and analyze patterns
20	550	3.MD.2	measure mass and volume and solve problems
21	B	3.NBT.3	multiply numbers by multiples of 10
22	D	3.MD.5	understand area measurement
23	160	3.MD.8	solve problems involving perimeter
24	$390 - 250$ $= 140$	3.OA.8	use estimation and rounding
25	B	3.OA.7	fluently multiply and divide
26	A	3.MD.7.b	use multiplication to find area
27	15	3.OA.3	use multiplication and division to solve problems
28	B	3.MD.1	write time and solve time problems
29	7	3.OA.4	solve multiplication and division equations
30	25, 10, 15	3.MD.3	draw picture and bar graphs and solve problems

Common Core Mathematics Practice Test, Session 2

Question	Answer	Standard	Skill Summary
31	B	3.OA.1	interpret products of whole numbers
32	4, 8, 16	3.NF.3.c	express whole numbers as fractions
33	A, E	3.OA.2	interpret quotients of whole numbers
34	4:20	3.MD.1	write time and solve time problems
35	C	3.OA.9	understand and use multiplication tables
36	80	3.OA.3	use multiplication and division to solve problems
37	B	3.MD.4	measure length and show data on line plots
38	C	3.NBT.1	round whole numbers
39	A	3.MD.2	measure mass and volume and solve problems
40	853	3.NBT.2	add and subtract whole numbers
41	8	3.MD.5	understand area measurement
42	20×6 120	3.MD.7.b	use multiplication to find area
43	$3, $24	3.OA.6	understand division as an unknown-factor problem
44	4, 8	3.NF.3.b	recognize and generate equivalent fractions
45	A	3.NF.3.a	understand equivalent fractions
46	A, C	3.G.2	partition shapes into parts and relate to fractions
47	14, 8, 15	3.MD.3	draw picture and bar graphs and solve problems
48	C	3.OA.8	solve word problems involving the four operations
49	$1\frac{3}{4}$	3.NF.2	represent fractions on a number line
50	B	3.OA.5	use properties of operations to multiply and divide
51	56	3.MD.5	understand area measurement
52	B, E	3.G.1	recognize, categorize, and analyze shapes
53	$\frac{1}{3}$	3.NF.3.d	compare fractions
54	4	3.OA.7	fluently multiply and divide
55	$(8 \times 3) + (2 \times 2)$ 28	3.MD.7.d	find the area of complex figures
56	12×1 6×2 3×4	3.OA.4	solve multiplication and division equations
57	A	3.NBT.3	multiply numbers by multiples of 10
58	192, 108	3.NBT.2	add and subtract whole numbers
59	E	3.MD.8	solve problems involving perimeter
60	2½	3.MD.2	measure mass and volume and solve problems

43